The Call of
the Clerihew

The Call of
the Clerihew

edited by Andy Jackson
and George Szirtes

Smokestack Books
1 Lake Terrace, Grewelthorpe, Ripon HG4 3BU
e-mail: info@smokestack-books.co.uk
www.smokestack-books.co.uk

ISBN 9781999674212

Smokestack Books
is represented
by Inpress Ltd

Contents

The Call of the Clerihew

Since we began the process of editing this book, we've been asked the same question on several occasions: *what is a clerihew?* If it's a poet asking the question, we sometimes explain by discussing form – rhyme scheme and metrical conventions. If anyone else asks, we have a few stock answers: the limerick's shorter, smarter sibling; an epic poem in four lines; a poetic takedown of the famous and celebrated. These slightly arch answers rarely clarify, so we usually resort to offering a few by way of illustration. Once we've recited three or four, most people cotton on pretty fast.

Some facts then: the clerihew was invented as a poetic form by Edmund Clerihew Bentley, a novelist and journalist writing as EC Bentley. His 1905 book *Biography for Beginners* introduced the clerihew to the world, and was followed up in later years by *More Biographies* and *Baseless Biographies*. Bentley died in 1956 after authoring some moderately successful detective novels, but it is the verse form that bears his name that cements his place in literary eternity.

The clerihew form is governed by some simple rules:

1. It must be four lines long
2. The rhyme scheme is AABB
3. Rhymes should be tight
4. Meter may vary across the four lines
5. The first line must be the name of the person about whom the clerihew is written

One of Bentley's best-known examples perfectly illustrates the form:

> Sir Christopher Wren
> Said, 'I am going to dine with some men.
> If anyone calls
> Say I am designing St. Paul's.'

As evidenced in the example above, a good clerihew is deeply satisfying. It will mix outrageous feats of rhyme with wilfully unregulated metre, surrealism and satire with occasional grains of factual accuracy. Many clerihews will make you smile; the very best will make you laugh out loud. The clerihew is light verse, true, but like all light verse, a good poet can elevate the form through skilful mastery of it, allied with wit, erudition and invention. Admit it: you're composing a clerihew of your own right now, aren't you?

Material for this book was assembled from responses to a series of prompts offered to a community of clerihew devotees on Facebook over several years. In translating the online project into a book, the biggest challenge was volume – around 4,000 clerihews were whittled down to the 800 or so that appear in these pages. The project was overseen by us as editors, both occasionally lauded to varying degrees as 'serious' poets, but both casualties of this most addictive of poetic intoxicants. Our strange addiction is shared by over seventy other contemporary poets, all masters of the form, to whom we are indebted for their enthusiasm and generosity in supporting this book.

Andy Jackson & George Szirtes
November 2018

Ancient Rome & Ancient Greece

Caesar Augustus
Said to his senators 'It's just us
That rule here. Well, actually
It's just me'.

Andy Jackson

Leonidas
Thought war a gas
And when the Persians acted sloppily
Things got hot at Thermopylae.

Andy Jackson

The Emperor Tiberius
Said 'You cannot be serious!
My dear Sejanus
You're talking out of your elbow.'

Judith Taylor

Tullus Aufidius
Looked hideous
In his new Roman sandals,
So he turned to the Vandals.

Robert Fitzmaurice

Homer
Deserves a diploma –
No silly ad
Interrupts the Iliad.

Tom Deveson

Leda
Was a keen reader.
She thought it was OK
To try out Swann's Way.

Tom Deveson

Socrates
Said 'Plato, please,
Write down what I says.
These are my last days.'

Joe Williams

Rhea
Would often go around *sans brassiere*
Which, for Cronus,
Was a bonus.

Andy Jackson

Martial
Was rather partial
To poems about kisses
On various orifices.

Tom Deveson

Constantine
Hit the Falernian wine
And said 'What we need
Is an Aposhtlesh' Creed.'

Sarah Walker

Romulus and Remus
Asked 'Who would deem us
More fit to rule Rome than any other?
Not with a wolf for a foster mother!'

Sarah Walker

The Empress Livia
Ignored such trivia
As whether Tiberius was in the room
And who in her family killed whom.

Tom Deveson

Coriolanus
Would have slain us
For mocking his cloaks,
Or making bum jokes.

Robert Fitzmaurice

Aristophanes
Would rest often. He's
The one by the willow,
With his head on a pillow.

Robert Fitzmaurice

Quintus Horatius Flaccus
Under the influence of Bacchus
Said: 'Lalage? Don't remember 'er!
Only her disjecta membra.'

Tom Deveson

Nero
Could go from zero
To nasty, it's reckoned,
In under one second.

Mark Totterdell

Claudius
Wasn't as bawdy as
Some of them. Though no saint,
He did show some restraint.

Mark Totterdell

Apuleius
Asked the players
Well versed in myth
'Does my ass look big in thith?'

Robert Fitzmaurice

Dionysus
Suffered a crisis
When he received a fax
Saying: 'Βρεκεκεκὲξ κοὰξ κοάξ.'

Tom Deveson

The Oracle at Delphi
Said 'Know thy selfie,'
And, whipping out her iPhon,
Took a lovely one with Python.

Tim Turnbull

The Emperor Domitian
Adjusted his position
Saying 'That was fine
But it's past the Year 69.'

Tom Deveson

Paris
Wore Harris
Tweed pants. He
Thus tickled Helen's fancy.

Jim Lindop

Cassandra?
I wouldn't want to slander her,
But she should give up the day job this minute
(I see no future in it).

Andy Jackson

Polyphemus
Was one of life's dreamers.
You'd guess that if you saw him
So keep an eye out for him.

Andy Jackson

Calypso
Said 'Odysseus is hip, so
I'll sing. Just the ticket!
Cricket Lovely Cricket.'

Tom Deveson

Plato
Said 'ToMAYto',
'ToMAHto' said Aristotle,
As they argued over the ketchup bottle.

Mark Totterdell

The Sirens
Sang a phrase of Byron's:
'Moussaka! Kleftiko! No price increase!
The Isles of Grease! The Isles of Grease!'

Tom Deveson

Athena
You should have seen her
In her younger days. Grand
Poster girl for the Olympian brand.

Andy Jackson

Medusa
Was a notorious boozer.
Although she usually drank alone,
It was the rest of us that got stoned.

Andy Jackson

Priam
I am
Reliably informed was a bit of a stud
Need a Trojan horse? He's got wood.

Andy Jackson

Sisyphus
Had a hissy fuss
When revealed as two-faced,
And was caught between a rock and a hard place.

Andy Jackson

The Cumaen Sibyl
Tended to dribble.
The Sibyl of Delphi
Was rather more healthy.

Sarah Walker

Pontius Pilate
Would turn several shades of violet
To learn that his reputation is so sordid
The way it's been recorded.

David Hill

Marcus Aurelius
Loved listening to Delius.
'On Hearing the First Cuckoo of Spring'
Was precisely his thing.

George Szirtes

Lucretius
Was seldom facetious.
There is nothing maturer
Than De Rerum Natura.

George Szirtes

'Caecilius
Est in horto'. Was it really as
Easy as that in
O-level Latin?

Mark Totterdell

Hades
Had an eye for ladies.
He lured them down there
Away from the fresh air.

Karen Margolis

'Cleopatra?
Her portraits don't flatter her.
She's a
Real beauty'. thought Caesar.

Mark Totterdell

Calgacus
Said 'Ye Romans cannae whack us!
We're covert in tattoos
An we're no feart o youse.'

Judith Taylor

Attila the Hun
Never owned a gun,
Which is why his wife
Did for him with a knife.

George Szirtes

Anti-colonials

Mahatma Gandhi
Was bandy,
And reminded me faintly
Of St Anthony, but more saintly.

George Szirtes

Pandit Nehru,
To be fair, you
Could have made a packet
If you'd patented that jacket.

Andy Jackson

Jomo Kenyatta
Considered politics a serious matter
And therefore refused to kowtow
To the Mau-Mau.

Andy Jackson

Kwame Nkrumah
Had a strange sense of humour.
He said: 'Me? The African Lenin?
I'd better build a jail with hundreds of men in.'

Tom Deveson

Mohammed Jinnah
Got his knickers in a
Twist and said 'Man!
I'd better get on and invent Pakistan.'

Andy Jackson

Artists

Georges Braque
Was on the right traque.
In seeking artistic veracity
He found he had a cubic capacity.

Andy Jackson

Grayson Perry
Was very
Quirky. Luck he spurned;
His fame was well-urned.

Andy Jackson

Pierre Renoir
Peignit la femme en forme de poire.
Mais Jean, son fils,
N'aimait pas cet artifice.

Alfred Corns

David Shrigley's
Lines could be wriggly.
Still, he got shortlisted for the Turner
Which is a nice little earner.

WN Herbert

Paul Cézanne
Had a revolutionary aesthetic plan:
'I'll go swimmin'
And paint lots and lots of naked women.'

Tom Deveson

William Holman Hunt
Made piety his stunt.
His works are peppered
With allusions to the Good Shepherd.

Tom Deveson

Henri Matisse
Said 'Art is War, not Peace!
I never throve
Until I became a fauve.'

Tom Deveson

Rembrandt van Rijn
Took a shijn
To his own face. In wanting to avoid scorn or
Ridicule, he painted himself into a corner.

Andy Jackson

Hans Arp
Heard his wife carp:
'You'll have to try much harder
If you want to become a Dada.'

Tom Deveson

Jasper Johns
Tried to sculpt in bronze,
But found unexpected snags:
'My attention just flags.'

Tom Deveson

Hieronymus Bosch
Had a face like a squash,
But when he painted starved peasants in terrible light,
It was an unearthly delight.

Rick Hilles

Tracey Emin
Is the gem in
Margate's pierced ear
Though some might sneer.

Sarah Walker

Paul Klee
Could not see
Why no-one could properly say
Paul Klee.

Andy Jackson

Artemisa Gentileschi
Painted no freschi
But lots of Judith, chopping off the head
Of the invader who tried to get her into bed.

Sarah Walker

Michelangelo Buonarotti
Woke up feeling grotty
Having painted an enormous fresco
For Tesco.

George Szirtes

Fra Filippo Lippi
Was kinda dippy
But succeeded in laying tons
Of nuns.

George Szirtes

Giotto
Was drunk, flat out, blotto.
And, much to be lamented,
His perfect circles looked dented.

George Szirtes

Claude Monet
Resisted all forms of donné.
When someone suggested he should paint the cathedral at Rheims,
He replied, 'In your dreams!'

George Szirtes

Banksy
Says 'Thanks'. He
Wants you all to know
He's thrilled. He just doesn't let it show.

Andy Jackson

Franz Hals
Had very few pals.
People laughed at his cavalier attitude, and how.
They're not laughing now.

Andy Jackson

Roy Lichtenstein
Is a favourite of mein,
Though I see no
Difference between his stuff and what's in *The Beano*.

Andy Jackson

Leo Baxendale
At any size'n'scale
Made Lichtenstein's oeuvre
Look frankly piss-pauvre.

Adam Horovitz

Kurt Schwitters
Terrified a circle of knitters
Into dropping stitches every week by breezing
Through the Fury of Sneezing.

Adam Horovitz

Damien Hirst
Must be the first
Artist whose entire career arc
Amounts to jumping the shark.

Mark Granier

Sir Anthony Caro
Professed himself an admirer of Camille Pissarro.
He may indeed be the smartest
Pissarro artist.

Jim Lindop

David Hockney
Wasn't a cockney,
But was known on the scene
As an old pearly queen.

Robert Fitzmaurice

Robert Hughes
Wrote an eloquent J'Accuse:
'Some contemporary art is expensive shite.'
Wow, was he right.

Tom Deveson

Edvard Munch,
No hunk
And no dream,
Ergo, scream.

Robert Fitzmaurice

Leonardo
Usually behaved with bravado,
But went into a panic
When people said 'Loved you in Titanic.'

Tom Deveson

Beryl Cook
Liked to make us look
At drinks and raucous jokes
Being enjoyed by well-rounded folks.

Sarah Walker

Pablo Picasso
Drank a lot of Brasso
Which gave his depictions of physiognomy
Autonomy.

WN Herbert

Mabel Lucie Attwell
Couldn't draw *that* well,
But fans of the twee
Might disagwee.

Colin West

Francis Bacon
Didn't like having his picture taken,
Unless the photographer made it cryptic
And preferably part of a triptych.

Robert Lindsay Marcus

Salvador Dali
Rode around on a Harley,
Then turned a bit stroppy
When its wheels went all floppy.

Mark Totterdell

Vincent Van Gogh
Gave a polite cough
When an American said 'So,
You must be Mr Van Gogh'.

Francis Moorcroft

Egon Schiele
Became too touchy-feele.
Vienna only recovered for sure
After that song by Midge Ure.

Beth McDonough

Francisco Goya:
What a lad for the soya!
Block-sinused in far Tipperary,
He swore off Bushmills and everything dairy.

Beth McDonough

Henry Moore
Saw his popularity soar
When folk took a poll
Of his work as a (w)hole.

Sue Barnard

William Blake
Refused a slice of cake:
'It's full of gluten,
And all the fault of Newton.'

Tom Deveson

Gustav Klimt
Rarely scrimped
On the gold leaf. In some works there ain't
Much space left for paint.

Mark Totterdell

MC Escher
Admitted, under pressure,
That if you fell down his stairs, you wouldn't stop
Till you hit the top.

Mark Totterdell

Praxiteles
Was famed for making cheese.
Nobody did it better
At making feta.

Graham Mummery

Pablo Picasso
Loved a lass so,
He immortalised her eyes and nose,
Even if he wasn't entirely sure where each bit goes.

Matthew Francis

Henry Fuseli
Was never put off his muesli
By the memory of a horse's head
Staring at him from the foot of the bed.

Matthew Francis

James McNeill Whistler
Was going to paint his sister,
But he thought 'Why bother?
I'll paint my mother.'

Francis Moorcroft

René Magritte,
Painter of apple-faced men and lace-up feet,
I come to praise, not to bury you:
This isn't a clerihew.

Matthew Francis

Marcus Johannes Vermeer
Said 'Stick this in your ear.'
'Only,' replied the girl,
'If I can keep the pearl.'

Robert Lindsay

Henri Rousseau
Said 'If you must scoff, then do so:
You won't laugh so hard
When I'm the toast of the avant-garde.'

Robert Lindsay Marcus

Leonardo Da Vinci
Said 'She's nice-looking, in't she!
But she found it a trial
When I said 'Try not to smile''

Robert Lindsay Marcus

Robert Motherwell
Was an artist like no other. Well-
Known for just doing a large splat,
But my 4-year-old could do that.

Andy Jackson

Canaletto
Isn't he finished yet? O
God, when is
He going to paint somewhere other than Venice?

Andy Jackson

John Constable
Thought 'If I paint a monster bull
In the foreground of The Hay Wain,
My reputation may wane.'

Mark Totterdell

Alfred Wallis
Found some solace
In the fact that his art wasn't thought too defective,
In spite of his failure to handle perspective.

Mark Totterdell

'Jackson Pollock's
Art is the absolute dog's bollocks.
Each paint drip packs an
Emotional punch,' opined one Pollock, Jackson.

Mark Totterdell

George Stubbs
Kept his paint in massive tubs,
Because, of course,
It took so much of it to paint a horse.

Mark Totterdell

Lucien Freud
Got quite annoyed
When critics went on about id
Just like his granddad did.

Robert Lindsay Marcus

Albrecht Dürer
Said 'I'd feel secürer
If I'd actually seen a rhino:
I mean, I think this is an accurate representation, but what do I know?'

Robert Lindsay Marcus

Gilbert & George
Made their works hard to forge
(And themselves rather wealthy)
Because each one's a selfie.

Robert Lindsay Marcus

Sir Antony Gormley
Was praised warmly
For each life-sized metal figure,
Though he did one with wings that was much, much bigger.

Mark Totterdell

Dante Gabriel Rossetti
Dropped his cigarette in his spaghetti.
The silly old Pre-Raphaelite
Nearly set the café alight.

Mark Totterdell

Edward Hopper
Could have come a cropper,
Had he called 'Nighthawks'
'Shitehawks'.

Mark Totterdell

Cy Twombly
Sighed sombrely,
'If only my art inspired as much fascination
As my extraordinary appellation.'

Robert Lindsay Marcus

Méret Oppenheim
Didn't put on her top in time,
So Man Ray
Snapped away.

Robert Lindsay Marcus

Bridget Riley?
Her work is rated highly,
Though all I get from it
Is a splitting headache and an urge to vomit.

Mark Totterdell

Australians

Kylie Minogue
Is ever in vogue,
Though the media seem less interested in her thoughts
Than her tiny shorts.

Andy Jackson

Clive James
Consigned to the flames
The writing he wasn't preserving for future ages.
That left thirty thousand pages.

Tom Deveson

Steve Irwin
Was forever stirrin'
It up with snakes and lizards.
With rays, he was less wizard.

Simon Williams

Germaine Greer
Had a bad year.
'It was the cruellest of crimes.
I was only on TV two hundred times.'

Tom Deveson

Errol Flynn,
With his cheeky grynn,
On pirate ships with decks awash
Buckled his swash.

Simon Williams

Dame Nellie Melba
Had many fans on Elba,
An island where she said 'The beach
Is a peach'.

Simon Williams

Howard Florey –
You know his Nobel story.
He developed penicillin
And the rest you can fill in.

Tom Deveson

Dame Joan Sutherland
Sang in many another land,
But they never said 'Return to Sender'
About La Stupenda.

Tom Deveson

Eric Bana
Has a mild manner.
He hardly ever throws a sulk,
Except when he is the Hulk.

Grant Tarbard

Russell Crowe
Doesnae know
Weer his accent's gannin.
No wonder Robin Hood received a panning.

Adam Horovitz

Ned Kelly
Was smelly,
And his armour plate
Had turned rusty of late.

Robert Fitzmaurice

Jason Donovan
Was one of an
Australian celebrity pair,
Should you care.

David Hill

Sir Lachlan McQuarrie
Was right to be sorry.
Without his hard work, Australia
Could have been a failure.

Jim Lindop

Sir Les Patterson
Said 'It doesn't matter son,
I've puked on so many shoes;
Just because they're the Queen's hardly makes it news?!'

Peadar O'Donoghue

Elle Macpherson
Has many attributes as a person.
It seems a bit shoddy
To call her just 'The Body.'

David Hill

Carry On Clerihewing

Charles Hawtrey
Had a thought: re
Fame's long idyll
'I was Private Widdle.'

Barton Young

Sid James
Often had characters with rude names.
But surely 'The Rumpo Kid' was a step too far?
...Ahyarhyarhyarhyarhyar.

Andy Jackson

Jim Dale
Was very stale.
'I'm misunderstood!'
No, you're balsa wood.

Grant Tarbard

Hattie Jacques
Was no great shakes
In roles of feminist sorority.
She had matronly authority.

Tom Deveson

Cartoon Characters

Judge Dredd
Under his helmet must have had a head,
But didn't once remove it
To prove it.

Andy Jackson

The Incredible Hulk,
In colour and bulk,
Sure as heck
Reminds me of Shrek.

Mark Totterdell

Spider-man,
Spider-man,
Insists on only rhyming
With himself while swinging and climbing.

Tim Turnbull

Wile E Coyote
Never learnt to float. He
Falls from cliffs impossibly steep,
To the echo of a distant 'meep, meep'.

Simon Williams

101 Dalmatians
And their defecations;
It's enough to make anyone feel
Like Cruella de Vil.

Mark Totterdell

Captain Pugwash
Said 'I should quash
The rumours that surround the names
Of Master Bates and Seaman Staines.'

Andy Jackson

Beryl the Peril –
Practically feral.
That's
Not counting the plaits.

Sarah Walker

Desperate Dan,
More bunkhouse than man,
Is expensive to employ; even at a buffet
It's a cow per pie per day.

Simon Williams

Daffy Duck
Always comes unstuck.
Every plan that Bugs knackers
Drives him quackers.

Adam Horovitz

Donald Duck
Would never cluck,
But then, in fact,
He seldom quacked.

Mark Totterdell

Goofy.
In truth he
Was in love with Mickey.
And Minnie. Tricky.

Adam Horovitz

Ivor the Engine
Should get an honourable mention;
Though slightly unconventional,
No-one could say he was two-dimensional.

Andy Jackson

Top Cat
Wasn't all that.
Close friends got to call him TC
Apparently.

Andy Jackson

Minnie the Minx
Consulted several shrinks:
'Since I was a nipper
I've LOVED my dad's slipper.'

Tom Deveson

Mrs Brady, Old Lady
Compared to Kate Adie,
Is equally Geordie
But significantly more bawdy.

Tom Deveson

Mickey Mouse?
Wouldn't have him in the house!
That awful squeaky voice!
He's gone. Rejoice!

George Szirtes

Superman
Didn't need a plan;
Alien messiah that he was,
He won the day, just coz.

Alvin Pang

The Pink Panther
Said 'Anther
Me thith' for the bee had stung
His tongue.

Robert Fitzmaurice

Popeye
Would occasionally drop by
With Olive wearing something skimpy,
And that dubious Mr Wimpy.

George Szirtes

Bod,
The little sod.
Here he comes,
Swinging his plums.

Robert Fitzmaurice

'Scooby-Doo'
Was a great show, true,
(Well it made me happy)
Till they brought in Scrappy.

Mark Totterdell

Steamboat Willie;
You'd look pretty silly,
I suppose,
If you had one of those.

Mark Totterdell

Fat Freddy's cat
Sat on the mat
Smoking a joint.
That was the point.

Karen Margolis

Pluto,
Soft howl sostenuto,
Gazed with the devotion of a Sufi
At Goofy.

David Hill

Woody Woodpecker;
Was he wooden? Was he heck! A
Rather annoying song, though, it's true.
'He-he-he-he-hu! He-he-he-he-hu!'

Andy Jackson

Noggin the Nog
Kept us all agog,
Though what was striking
Was how little raping and pillaging he did for a Viking.

Mark Totterdell

Nogbad The Bad
Was said to be mad
That Noggin was made king
For he wasn't cut out for that sort of thing.

Andy Jackson

Mr Benn
Now and then
Tried gender-swapping
Instead of magical shopping.

Adam Horovitz

Olive Oyl
Was merely a foil,
With a terrible image
One down from spinach.

George Szirtes

Prince Charming?
Quite alarming.
Without makeup
No wake up.

Adam Horovitz

'Wallace and Gromit';
Gromit might have taken from it
Some solace,
Had it been called 'Gromit and Wallace'.

Mark Totterdell

Bash Street's Teecher
Concurred with Nietzsche
That Wilfred's green-jumpered unfathomable stare
Exemplified *Ewige Wiederkehr*.

Tom Deveson

Rufus Roughcut
Looked incredibly buff, but
Even from afar
He smelt like a tart's boudoir.

Tim Turnbull

Professor Pat Pending
Was sad at the ending
Of the way out Wacky Races
But they all keep in touch (in most cases).

Paul McGrane

Penelope Pitstop,
Don't be a nit, stop
Squealing, persist.
The Hooded Claw would run scared from a feminist.

Adam Horovitz

The Ant Hill Mob
Had just one job;
Protecting Penelope was their goal
(Although that was supposed to be Peter Perfect's role).

Andy Jackson

The Great Grape Ape
Didn't fly or wear a cape,
But if you wanted a 40-foot purple gorilla who liked to travel
around on top of a dog's car,
You didn't have to look far.

David Hill

Tintin
Kept hintin'
To Haddock, again and again,
That he liked bearded men.

Mark Totterdell

Walt Disney
Is off his head, isn'e?
What could be crazier
Than Fantasia?

Mark Totterdell

Pinocchio,
I claim, came from Tokyo,
Though as I speak I grow a jokey nose
Just like Pinocchio's.

Mark Totterdell

Viz
Is
Like the Beano
But more obscene, oh!

Mark Totterdell

Winnie the Pooh;
Does he do
What his name suggests he should?
Does a bear shit in the Hundred Acre Wood?

Mark Totterdell

Dennis the Menace
Was useless at tennis,
But his racket
Made DC Thompson a packet.

Anne Berkeley

Lord Snooty
Loved to shake his public school booty.
If that made the totty randy
Well, that was Dandy.

Andy Jackson

Cowboys & Indians

Tom Mix
Was the king of Cowboy flicks.
When it came to the Old West,
He was the original, and best.

Andy Jackson

Bronco Layne
On the Texas plain.
He was quite hot.
I fancied him a lot.

Sharon Larkin

Kit Carson
Was arrested for arson.
He burned an Indian village right through,
So they decided to Sioux.

Tom Deveson

Champion the Wonder Horse
Was rarely found on a course.
Since being struck down with mange,
He was more at home on the range.

Andy Jackson

Hopalong Cassidy
Suffered from stomach acid. He
Resorted to Snake Oil and Dr J Collis-Browne's Chlorodyne
To help him feel fine.

Jim Lindop

Cochise
Was so obese,
His nickname was 'Bum of the great plains buffalo!'
'Well,' as my Mum would have said, 'it just goes to show!'

Jim Lindop

Jack Palance
Did not shoot Liberty Valance.
Nor did Jimmy Stewart. It was John Wayne
Again.

Jim Lindop

Sitting Bull
Was out on the pull,
But the squaws poured scorn
On his Little Big Horn.

Andy Jackson

Wyatt Earp
Was a little twerp,
But, hey,
His Corral was OK.

Mark Totterdell

The Milky Bar Kid,
Whatever he did,
Responsibility for those travesties of the Wild West lay
With Nestlé.

Mark Totterdell

'Tonto,
Come pronto!'
Squeaked the Lone Ranger –
Who of late had turned stranger.

Robert Fitzmaurice

'Hiawatha';
If you believe its author
To be anyone but Longfellow,
You've got the wrong fellow.

Mark Totterdell

Butch Cassidy,
Remained placid. He
Never got angry, though The Sundance Kid
Often did.

Andy Jackson

Wild Bill Hickok
Had a very thick cock.
(But then, when did you ever
Meet a chicken who's clever?)

Mark Totterdell

Geronimo
Said 'Hang on a mo.
What do people have to gain
By shouting my name when they jump from a plane?'

Mark Totterdell

Buffalo Bill,
Found horse-riding a thrill,
But it was even more nice on
A bison.

Mark Totterdell

'Jane,'
Said Wild Bill Hickok, 'you're a pain!'
'Damn it,' he
Continued, 'you're a calamity!'

Mark Totterdell

The Man With No Name
Used to proclaim
That 'The Man with No Name' was what he was called.
'Though it's not actually my name,' he drawled.

Mark Totterdell

Roy Rogers'
Todger's
Not as big as
Trigger's.

Mark Totterdell

Dead Pop Stars

Buddy Holly -
Just one piece of folly.
He'll never take that plane
Again.

George Szirtes

Hot Lips Page
Was all the rage.
He was only forty-six years old
When his lips went cold.

George Szirtes

Kurt Cobain:
His life was a hurricane.
His feedback unconfined,
Oh well, whatever, nevermind.

Grant Tarbard

Ray Edward Cochrane
Suffered fatal injuries to the brain.
A short life and far from steady
For Cochran, Eddie.

George Szirtes

Brian Jones
Never made old bones.
You shouldn't fool
With a swimming pool.

Tom Deveson

Elvis
Shook his pelvis,
But that last deep-fried Mars Bar
Was one Mars Bar too far.

Peadar O'Donoghue

Sid Vicious,
His id pernicious,
At least died before he could utter:
'I can't believe it's not butter.'

Robert Fitzmaurice

Marc Bolan
Had his jeep stolen.
Bad news. It was dark
And he was in Jurassic Park.

Robert Fitzmaurice

Cliff Richard
And a witch had
Pulled off quite a coup
Considering he died in 1992.

Robert Fitzmaurice

Sandy Denny
Had admirers many
For Fotheringay and Fairport Convention.
She never drew a pension.

Simon Williams

Phil Everly
Smoked too heavily.
Now he's somewhere above,
Singing Bye Bye Love.

Simon Williams

Pigpen
Wasn't like other men.
He was misled
Into being one of the un-Grateful Dead.

Grant Tarbard

Bob Marley
Made you look a proper Charlie
If you tried to get him in a headlock;
You'd just end up with dreadlock.

Mark Totterdell

Elmore James
Had the juke joints in flames;
There was no elbow room
When he played 'Dust My Broom'.

Grant Tarbard

Ian Curtis
Found that hurt is
Enough to destroy;
Deep Division, no Joy.

Mark Totterdell

Patsy Cline
Snorted a line
And said 'I get the words kinda hazy,
When I drink & sing 'Crazy'.'

Grant Tarbard

Amy Winehouse:
Shame she didn't find nous
And stay on track.
Now she's gone back to black.

Rachel Rooney

Keith Relf
Electrocuted himself
With his own guitar;
The most rock'n'roll death by far!

Mark Totterdell

Stumpy Joe,
What a way to go!
The only fictional drummer ever known
To choke on vomit that wasn't his own.

Mark Totterdell

Syd Barrett
Hid in a garret
For years after being made unemployed
By Pink Floyd.

Mark Totterdell

Farrokh Bulsara
Put on mascara
And said 'Now I'm ready,
Please call me Freddie!'

Mark Totterdell

Peter Tosh?
Gosh!
What?
Shot!

Mark Totterdell

Screaming Lord Sutch
Is remembered as much
For losing elections
As for his music's imperfections.

Mark Totterdell

Jeff Buckley
Unluckily
Drowned. (Was that him
Or Tim?)

Mark Totterdell

Lou Reed
When forced to concede,
Said 'Heaven? Hell, no! Indulge me, messieurs –
I'll take Venus, in furs.'

Shauna Robertson

John Bonham.
Any drugs going, you'd imagine he'd be on 'em,
Though in fact it was vodka, neat,
That put a stop to his beat.

Mark Totterdell

Eddie Kendricks
Wasn't Hendrix,
Although, it must be said,
He's just as dead.

Mark Totterdell

Joe Strummer
Strummed a guitar, he wasn't a drummer.
Was nominative determinism to blame
Or was it an assumed name?

Mark Totterdell

Richards and Jagger;
What staggers is how they still swagger,
Instead
Of being dead.

Mark Totterdell

Brian Jones
Was one of the Stones
Who took drugs and drank
And, like a stone, sank.

Mark Totterdell

John Entwistle
Would tunelessly blow a bent whistle
When too off his face
To play bass.

Mark Totterdell

Wolfman Jack
Had a heart attack.
(It's not every time
That name and death rhyme.)

Mark Totterdell

John Lennon
Could put his pen on
A fine tune. Oh, joy,
But did you read the news today? Oh Boy!

Peadar O'Donoghue

Prince
Makes me wince
I hear the little twerp'll
Only dress in purple.

Mark Totterdell

Despots

Kim Jong-Un:
Bit of a wrong 'un,
Though being the subject of a personality cult could prove
To be a good Korea move.

Andy Jackson

'Bashar al-Assad.
Is the man good or bad?'
Is an examination question
Designed to ruin your digestion.

George Szirtes

Benito Mussolini
Had a teeny-weeny
Thingy, so in spite of all that lamppost stuff you may recall,
He actually wasn't well hung at all.

Mark Totterdell

Francisco Franco
Cleaned his uniform with Blanco,
In the hope it would appeal
To the *Guardia Civil.*

Tom Deveson

King Farouk
Issued a rebuke:
'Politics? Not in the mood –
Just more women and more food.'

Tom Deveson

Baby Doc Duvalier
Was known for his esprit d'escalier.
All the arguments he felt he'd lost
Were later analysed for smart ripostes.

Jim Lindop

Louis Seize and Marie Antoinette
Would drink champagne and, later, for a bet,
(Not that they were short of dosh)
Would force the peasantry to eat brioche.

Jim Lindop

Colonel Gaddafi
Was never heard to laugh. He
Ruled Libya with an iron fist
But isn't much missed.

Andy Jackson

Jim Jones
(God curse his bones)
Didn't intend to be cruel,
Though the Aid he administered was not Kool.

Andy Jackson

Napoleon Bonaparte
Watched the Imperial Guard at Waterloo get blown apart.
He stopped, stood stunned, staggered and stared,
And said *O merde!*

Tom Deveson

Gnaeus Julius Agricola
Was an Imperial stickler.
He said 'Caledonia's too big to police
So I'll make it a wilderness and call it peace.'

Tom Deveson

Pol Pot
Said 'You will be shot
For disagreeing with me.'
Humanely adding 'Would you like some tea?'

Graham Mummery

Frederick Barbarossa
Got crossa and crossa
With people thinking he was weird
Because of the beard

Judith Taylor.

Lady Bathory
Was a bit like a Tory
In that she wet her tongue
In the blood of the young.

Bethany W Pope

Maximilien de Robespierre
Wore ladies' underwear.
He said it was an error
Caused by the reign of terror.

Brian Kirk

Tamerlane
Watched a crane
Slowly cross the sky.
17 million would die.

Robert Fitzmaurice

Augusto Pinochet
Was not killed by a ricochet
From a bullet fired in rage.
He died in old age.

George Szirtes

Catherine the Great
Never did have that date
With the horse. She died very old,
With plenty of gold.

Bethany W Pope

Nicolae Ceauşescu
Hoped someone would come to his rescue,
But after all his diabolical work he
Ended up a Christmas turkey.

David Hill

Vlad
Had
Those he disliked
Spiked.

David Hill

Kim Jong-Il
Invented the pneumatic drill.
He was also said to come up with the Tommy Gun.
Oh no, that was his son.

Grant Tarbard

Des Pot
Didn't think a lot
Of his unfortunate name.
Still, he stuck with it all the same.

Peadar O'Donoghue

EC Bentley

Edmund Clerihew Bentley
Wrote comic verses, gently
Lampooning the rich and the famous,
And making us smile. Who can blame us?

Beth Somerford

Edmund Clerihew Bentley
Wrote 'Trent's Last Case' intently,
But his bigger claim to fame
Is the verse-form which bears his name.

Sue Barnard

Edmund Clerihew Bentley
Went into that good night quite gently.
Instead of wailings and boo-hoos
He left behind him Clerihews.

Sarah Walker

Edmund Clerihew Bentley
Started at The Times puzzle intently.
'Not a crossed word shall pass my lips
Until I've had my fish and chips.'

Grant Tarbard

Edmund Clerihew Bentley
Insisted – though gently –
That when you use his form
You adhere to the norm.

Tom Deveson

Philip Trent
Was created by EC Bent-
ley, but very few
Are those who'd mistake a classic whodunit for a clerihew.

Mark Totterdell

Bentley (Edmund Clerihew)
Wrote comic verses, but very few
About Walter Mitty –
Which is a pity.

Beth Somerford

Easy Listening

Mantovani
Told me a good yarn. He
Once picked up a nasty infection
From someone in his string section.

Andy Jackson

Perry Como
Was the major-domo,
Though Edmundo Ros
Thought HE was bos.

Andy Jackson

The Swingle Singers
Were such mingers
That nobody would mingle
With a single Swingle.

Mark Totterdell

James Last
Just couldn't be arsed.
If he wasn't the worst,
He'd have been called James First.

Mark Totterdell

Richard Clayderman
Would never pay the man,
Which is a fine way
To treat someone who comes to tune your Steinway.

Andy Jackson

The Boston Pops?
I hope it stops.
It's easy
To make me queasy.

Mark Totterdell

Henry Mancini
Found it a teeny
Bit hard to forgive a
Person who confused 'Moon Panther' with 'The Pink River'.

Mark Totterdell

Nat King Cole
Was a peaceable soul.
His weapon of choice
Was his mellifluous voice.

Sarah Walker

Tony Bennett
Cried when it
Became clear at the disco
He'd left his heart in San Francisco.

Robert Fitzmaurice

Val Doonican
Could really croon. He can
Still be found today in fans' letters,
And a vast wardrobe of sweaters.

Robert Fitzmaurice

Bing
Really could sing,
But what a hash
With Stills and Nash.

Peadar O'Donoghue

Barry Manilow
Tinkles on the piannah, though
It's a talent, I suppose,
For which he has a nose.

Heather Fiona Reid

Explorers & Adventurers

Scott of the Antarctic
Found coming second cathartic,
Preferring the lesser regalia
Of heroic failure.

Andy Jackson

Bear Grylls
Loves thrills.
Who cares
That he grills bears?

Mark Totterdell

Tenzing and Hillary
Opened a distillery;
After reaching the top,
They could do with a drop.

Tom Deveson

An Unknown Tribe
Discovered America. No scribe
Recorded the date.
And now it's a bit too late.

Bethany W Pope

Captain James Cook,
In my book,
Must be considered a failure
For discovering Australia.

Mark Totterdell

Leif Erikson
Got a fit of the hysterics on
Discovering Vinland, screaming 'I'm a Viking
And this dump is not to my liking.'

Andy Jackson

Sir Richard Burton
Was never certain
If he was exploring the Nile
Or taking Liz Taylor up the aisle.

Tom Deveson

Captain James Cook
Always took a look
At his map before setting out
Then drew his own if he had any doubt.

Graham Mummery

Sir Ranulph Twisleton-Wykeham-Fiennes
Pines
For a shorter name –
Just signing his own books drives him insane.

Graham Mummery

Vasco de Gama
Liked a bit of drama
And would appear with tights on
Before turning the lights on.

George Szirtes

TE Lawrence,
Whilst travelling through Florence,
Developed a taste for Chianti,
And the complete works of Dante.

Jim Lindop

Afanasiy Nikitin
Always took his bikkie tin.
Though frequently drunk
He still liked to dunk.

George Szirtes

George Mallory
Took no salary.
That is why he eschewed
Wearing clothes, and travelled in the nude.

Graham Mummery

Sir Walter Raleigh
Did not ride a Raleigh.
Very few pirates like
Being seen on a bike.

George Szirtes

Captain Oates
Floats
In memory like Scott
Does not.

Robert Fitzmaurice

Captain George Vancouver
Managed to manoeuvre
His ship along the Pacific
Coast (Alaska, British Columbia, Washington and Oregon, to
be specific).

Mark Totterdell

Ernest Shackleton
Always took Yakult on
His trips, because every explorer
Needs healthy gut flora.

Mark Totterdell

Ray Mears
Knows no fears.
In the matter of survival
He has no rival.

Sue Barnard

Henry Hudson
Said to the first mate 'It's no good, son;
Your villainous mutiny
Will not stand up to scrutiny.'

Andy Jackson

Captain Bligh
Sighed 'Oh my!
It's certainly a misty un!'
And didn't see the knife in the hand of Mr Christian.

Harry Gallagher

Ferdinand Magellan
Said 'The world is my melon!'
But such optimism didn't amount to a hill of beans
When he got to the Philippines.

Robert Lindsay Marcus

Christopher Columbus
Killed natives in vast numbers.
He may have impressed Isabella,
But he wasn't a very nice fella.

Robert Lindsay Marcus

Tristão da Cunha,
I wouldn't impunha;
I'm glad you're on dry land,
For no man is an island.

Andy Jackson

Marco Polo
Retired from travelling solo
To invent both a posh horsy sport
And a mint of the centreless sort.

Mark Totterdell

Sir Francis Drake
Comments during bowling mini-break:
'The Spanish armada?
Nada.'

Nigel Parke

Thor Heyerdahl
Said 'My raft'll go further than a hire car'll,
Though a Ford Focus might be less creaky
Than the Kon-Tiki.'

Robert Lindsay Marcus

Mungo Park
Lost his adventurous spark.
'Oh, where did all the fun go?'
Sighed Mungo.

Mark Totterdell

Erik the Red
Always said
'Greenland wasn't there before I found it.
All the others must just have sailed around it!'

Jim Lindop

Henry Morton Stanley
Was really tough and manly,
While David Livingstone, it's generally agreed,
Was a bit of a weed.

Mark Totterdell

Amerigo Vespucci
Always wore Gucci.
He remarked that nothing was horrider
Than the shirts they wore in Florida.

Jim Lindop

Intellectuals

John Maynard Keynes
Was forever causing scenes.
Milton Friedman
Told him 'There's no need, man.'

Andy Jackson

John Kenneth Galbraith
Had plenty of faith
That he could do real economics
And write witty lines suitable for both presidents and comics.

Graham Mummery

Claude Levi-Strauss
Often left his house
Using devious means
To avoid people queuing to buy his jeans.

Graham Mummery

CP Snow
Kept in tow
A couple of vultures
While pecking at two cultures.

Graham Mummery

Kurt Gödel
Makes my blood curdle.
I tried to read his paper 'The Consistency of the Axiom of
Choice and of the Generalized Continuum Hypothesis with
the Axioms of Set Theory' for a minute
But couldn't see any logic in it.

Andy Jackson

Carl Jung
Said 'I have flung
Out this obsession with sex.' This especially annoyed
Sigmund Freud.

Graham Mummery

Alan Watts
Drank lots. And lots.
But still knew how
To ride the Tao.

Shauna Robertson

Bertrand Russell
Couldn't resist the rustle of a bustle.
His philosophy embraced such fun
And the mathematics of one and one.

Joan Lennon

Alain de Botton
Has forgotten
Far more than you
Or I ever knew.

Mark Totterdell

Aleister Crowley
Was interested solely
In drugs, buggery and other forms of abuse.
The black magic was just an excuse.

James Sutherland Smith

Roland Barthes
Is a pompous old farthes.
Either he stops holding forth, or
I shall bring about the death of the author.

Judi Sutherland

Michel Foucault
Said 'It's nobody's fault.
How were you to know
It's pronounced 'Foucault'?'

Andy Jackson

Friedrich Nietzsche
Was a very poor teacher.
When he said 'What doesn't kill you makes you stronger'
He couldn't have been wronger.

Judi Sutherland

Camille Paglia,
I hear you're keeping a tally? A
List of sexist clerihew writers has you snarling?
Get back in the kitchen, darling.

Andy Jackson

Malcolm Muggeridge
Annoyed me to buggerage,
Particularly when he started decryin'
Monty Python's Life of Brian.

Simon Williams

George Steiner
Wrote the finer
Points of tragedy are in the odium
Of the podium.

Robert Fitzmaurice

Marcel Proust
May have known the *mot juste*
But he wrote too many pages when
He dunked that pesky madeleine.

Judi Sutherland

Jonathan Miller
Said 'Thumbs up to Schiller,
But golly,
That Schopenhauer was off his trolley.'

Robert Fitzmaurice

AC Grayling
Has only one failing –
He offers no relief
From his self-belief.

Tom Deveson

Goethe
Said to young Werther:
'Your schnitzel appears cursed.
Still, hope for the best, but prepare for the wurst.'

Robert Fitzmaurice

Sigmund Freud,
Never more overjoyed
Than when sitting on his bum
Blaming his mum.

Harry Gallagher

Ezra Pound
Is no longer around.
But due to the financial downturn, you see
We're now down to Ezra 50p.

Andy Jackson

James Bond

Auric Goldfinger
Ended up as an old singer.
He took the risk
In search of a gold disc.

Andy Jackson

Q
Had been 'One of the Few.'
M,
One of them.

Jim Lindop

Dr No
Meets The Story Of O?
Well, I guess
We could call it Dr Yes...

Mark Granier

Sean Connery
Deserves no honour. He
Talks vicious crap
About giving women a slap.

Tom Deveson

Honey Ryder
Tried to confide her
Deepest secrets in James Bond.
She soon rose out of his shallow pond.

Adam Horovitz

Rosa Klebb
Caught Bond in her web;
But Connery said: 'SMERSH?
I've dealt with wersh.'

Tom Deveson

Diana Rigg
Got the Bond girl gig
And proved that Bond and marriage
Go together like a hearse and carriage.

Adam Horovitz

Jill St John
Said 'You turn me on.
But keep your proper place
Just in Case.'

Tom Deveson

Dr Kananga
Was played with anger.
Felix Leiter
Kept it tighter.

Andy Jackson

Tatia Romanova?
I wasn't a fan of her,
But Plenty O'Toole
Made me drool.

Andy Jackson

Solitaire
Had quite a flair
For Tarot. Kananga treated her severely.
She should have seen it coming, really.

Simon Williams

Desmond Llewelyn
As boffin was well in,
But was driven to distraction
By directors shouting 'Cue, Action!'

Simon Williams

James Bond
Is over-fond
Of luxury brands
And national-security-threatening one-night stands.

Anne Berkeley

Dick Van Dyke
Is the Bond actor I most like.
Fighting Gert Fröbe with a versatile car
And a fantasy name for his female co-star.

David Hill

Donald 'Red' Grant
Said 'I don't care, I can't
Drink white wine with fish:
That stuff tastes like pish.

Judith Taylor

George Lazenby?
Let this his blazon be:
'Sometimes longevity
Hinges on brevity.'

David Hill

Roger Moore:
Pussy Galore
Is what I should have done
When I was twenty-one.

Paul McGrane

Miss Moneypenny
Wasn't getting any
From 00-yes-maybe-don't-know
So she married Dr No.

Adam Horovitz

Daniel Craig?
A plague
On all his houses. No Bond
Should ever be blond.

Andy Jackson

Pussy Galore
Knew the score.
At the chance of a double entendre
Fleming was not one to squandre.

Harry Gallagher

007,
A match made in Heaven;
If there's an honorary
Award, present it to Shir Shean Connery.

Erik Zoha

M
Said 'Ahem,
Bond, you've been killing men.
Again.'

Francis Moorcroft

Ernst Stavro Blofeld's fluffy white cat,
While being stroked, complained that
Blofeld had an even more cold finger
Than Auric Goldfinger.

Mark Totterdell

Scaramanga
Should not be confused with Dr Kananga,
And neither of them is the kangaroo
In 'Winnie the Pooh'.

Mark Totterdell

Timothy Dalton
You couldn't pin a fault on,
Except for playing it so strait-laced –
Less debonair, more po-faced.

Harry Gallagher

Jazz Musicians

Tommy Dorsey
Was king of the trombone of course. He
Made each song a jazz hymn
(Now I'm Getting A Little Sentimental Over Him).

Andy Jackson

Acker Bilk
Was the best known of the trad ilk,
Always looking happy as Larry, yet
Lonely was the lilt of his clarinet.

Andy Jackson

John Coltrane
Put the audience under strain.
Can you listen with aplomb
To Om?

Tom Deveson

Dave Brubeck,
Famed from Lima to Lubeck,
Deserves more
Lines than four,
So I'll take five.

Mark Totterdell

Thelonious Monk
Went Kerplink-Pause-Kerplunk,
Playing the eponymous blues in B flat
And wearing a silly hat.

Tom Deveson

Charlie Parker
Had a darker
Side, saying 'Everybody has,
But that's jazz.'

Andy Jackson

Chris Barber
Would often harbour
A wish to be less trad,
Dad.

Andy Jackson

Charles Mingus
Took his fingers
Off his bass
And punched Jimmy Knepper in the face.

Mark Totterdell

Cab Calloway
Whisked a gal away,
Saying 'You and I have a great future,
Minnie the Moocher!'

Mark Totterdell

Count Basie
And His Band drove Kansas City crazy,
So much so that musicians in Chicago
Considered an embargo.

Jim Lindop

Duke Ellington
Rarely wore wellington
Boots,
Preferring sharp suits.

Mark Totterdell

Miles Davis
Likes to shave his
Chin, unlike Bix Beiderbecke
Who has too wide a neck.

Andy Jackson

Stéphane Grappelli
Sent a telegram saying 'Can't play tonight. Watching telly.'
An unconvinced Dizzy Gillespie
Replied 'You'd best be.'

Andy Jackson

George Melly
Sported a belly
But there wasn't an ounce of fat
Under that suave man's hat.

Robert Fitzmaurice

Literary Characters

Macduff
Was tough
On death and the causes of death,
Unlike Macbeth.

George Szirtes

'Sherlock Holmes
And the Case of the Priapic Garden Gnomes'
Has never been aired;
The world is not yet prepared.

Mark Totterdell

Jane Eyre
Knew not from where
All her troubles came forth.
It's grim up north.

Shauna Robertson

Professor Moriarty
Held a musical party;
They played on paper and combs
'There's No Police Like Holmes.'

Tom Deveson

Godot,
More 'NO NO NO!
Oh good God, no!'
Than 'Good oh!'

Peadar O'Donoghue

Heathcliff
Said 'If
I'd only had some early mothering,
These heights wouldn't seem so wuthering.'

Tom Deveson

Emma
Presented Mr Knightley with a dilemma:
'She has a tendency towards kitsch,
But she's handsome, clever and rich.'

Tom Deveson

Miss Marple
Was never heard to carp. Pull
Her in and she'll smell a rat,
The interfering old bat.

Andy Jackson

Fanny Price
Hoped it would be nice
Taking off her knickers
For Edmund, most boring of vicars.

Tom Deveson

Winston Smith
Sobbed 'It's a myth
That two and two make four.
Big Brother knows the score.'

Tom Deveson

Paul Morell
Said 'Bloody hell,
I want to come out as gay
But what would me mother say?'

Andy Jackson

Mr Kurtz
Got his just desserts.
He had horror in his head.
Then he dead.

Tom Deveson

Fitzwilliam Darcy
Went too far. See
Him emerge dripping from the lake, look!
(Though technically that wasn't in the book).

Andy Jackson

Lady Chatterley
Said 'Things have been good latterly.
I can't believe my luck –
Mellors wants a kiss.'

Tom Deveson

Sebastian Flyte
After many a drunken day and night
And needing a strict warder
Joined the Ursine Order.

Tom Deveson

Othello
Is a violent fellow.
Desdemona sings 'Willow Willow Willow.'
He raves 'Pillow Pillow Pillow.'

Tom Deveson

Gollum
Could write a whole column
On the perils of letting what seems precious
Enmesh us.

Mark Totterdell

Tess
Was forced to acquiesce
When Alec
Became phallic.

Tom Deveson

Gabriel Oak
Soon goes broke,
But Bathsheba Everdene
Is a walking cash machine.

Tom Deveson

Biggles
Never wiggles.
He just reveals
His nerves of steel.

Simon Williams

'Robinson Crusoe,
You've been through so
Many adventures, haven't you?
...Tell us about disc number two.'

Mark Totterdell

Christopher Robin
Saddled up his trusty steed, Dobbin,
To ride to the A & E near the Palace,
Because he had gone down with Alice.

Jim Lindop

Nicholas Nickleby
Rode an old bicycle. He
Coveted a Chopper
Which was only right and proper.

Andy Jackson

Tom Pinch
Doesn't get into a clinch.
You have to be wary
Of misreading his encounter with Mary.

Tom Deveson

Uriah Heep:
Such a creep.
Let's all give a sigh
For 'umble pie.

Karen Margolis

Bill Sikes?
Yikes!
Whatever did Nancy
Find to fancy?

Mark Totterdell

Sir Leicester
Can't identify Esther
Because Lady Dedlock
Had – heaven forfend! – sex before wedlock.

Tom Deveson

Pip
Hoped to unzip
His beloved Estella.
But that happened in a different novella.

Tom Deveson

Movie Directors

Michael Bay
Is oft heard to say
'Sod Sturm und Drang,
Let's have another bang.'

Andy Jackson

Joseph L Mankiewicz
Decided to make a swanky pitch
To Producers, which helped him achieve
All About Eve.

Andy Jackson

Oliver Stone:
I guess we should have known –
The plot is always the same:
Carnage. The Government's to blame.

Andy Jackson

David Lynch
May be regarded as a genius, at a pinch,
Though there's always some doubt
As to what his films are about.

Mark Totterdell

Lars von Trier
Came up with Dogme 95 and Dogville. I fear
That the only way to explain
Is that he's actually a Great Dane.

Mark Totterdell

Guy Ritchie?
I don't want to sound bitchy,
But the awfulness of his films is hard to credit.
(But please don't tell him that I said it).

Mark Totterdell

Alfred Hitchcock,
No matter which cock-
And-bull story he was directing, would appear in it
For a minute.

Mark Totterdell

Pier Paolo Pasolini
Fingered the linguine
And said to the monk and the rabbit
'Mama Mia, that's a filthy habit.'

Robert Fitzmaurice

Roger Vadim?
Loads of lovely ladies 'ad 'im!
Apart from Brigitte Bardot
There were many others that I don't know.

Jim Lindop

Wim Wenders
Mag nicht benders:
'Die angels solten sip sip sip
Und dancers skip skip skip.'

Robert Fitzmaurice

Ken Russell
Chortled 'What a fuss'll
I stir up with each naked nun.
This could be fun!'

Mark Totterdell

Marc Forster and Nick Park
Tried co-directing for a lark.
What came from it
Was 'Quantum of Wallace and Gromit.'

Mark Totterdell

Steve McQueen
Can sometimes be seen
To be rather unflinching:
Starvation, loveless sex and lynching.

Sarah Walker

Ridley Scott
Got
Anti-mammalian
In Alien.

Simon Williams

Stephen Frears
Had tiny little ears
Into which he inserted Orton's prick.
It was his party trick.

George Szirtes

Peter Greenaway
Had hardly been away
A week when rumours ran rife
About the cook, the thief, the lover and his wife.

George Szirtes

Richard Lester
Was prepared to let things fester
And rarely felt bright
After a hard day's night.

George Szirtes

Ken Loach
Advocated a socially conscious approach
And was rarely esoteric
Apart from in Looking for Eric.

George Szirtes

Russ Meyer
I can't help but admire.
I don't care what other people say –
He has his knockers, but I think he's okay.

Andy Jackson

Bela Tarr
Is the best, by far
At the slow examination
Of a whole Damnation.

Rachel Rooney

Fritz Lang
Wasn't part of the gang.
Hitler was quick to condemn
M.

Andy Jackson

Tod Browning's
Crowning
Achievement, as far as it went
Was a Freak event.

Andy Jackson

Terrence Malick
Was a Smart Alec
But Ed Wood
Was no bloody good.

Andy Jackson

Pedro Almodavar
Crossed a bridge too far
With broken embraces
In strange Spanish places.

Sue Kindon

John Ford
Of his own accord
Took the Stagecoach instead of the train –
Thereby inventing John Wayne.

George Szirtes

Akira Kurosawa
Is getting angrier by the hour.
Hollywood keeps stealing his ideas without giving him any credit.
There, I've said it.

Andy Jackson

Wim Wenders
Simply adored Eastenders:
High art was fine, he said, but soaps were higher,
As is perfectly obvious from Wings of Desire.

George Szirtes

John Cassavetes
Responded to Hollywood's entreaties
And directed movies till it hurt. He
Made a few Dozen, only one of which was Dirty.

Andy Jackson

Frederico Fellini
Was fond of the old Martini.
When asked what his limit was, for a laugh,
He replied 'Eight and a half.'

Andy Jackson

Joel and Ethan Coen,
It is little known,
Were fans of The Good Life, which is why Fargo
Is dedicated to Margo.

George Szirtes

Nicholas Roeg
Is often in vogue.
That one in Venice gave me a scare.
(Don't look now, but he's over there.)

Andy Jackson

Mel Brooks,
You're not blessed with looks,
But your wife just goosed me!
Is she trying to seduce me?

Andy Jackson

Ernst Lubitsch
Exclaimed 'You bitch!
I'll never vork mit you again, Greta!'
And then he ate her!

George Szirtes

Sergio Leone
Preferred Spaghetti Westerns to macaroni.
His last film was Once Upon A Time in America (1984).
He'd have carried on if he'd had a few dollars more.

Andy Jackson

Ken Loach,
Wanting always to appear beyond reproach,
Renounced his stories
And joined the Tories.

Jim Lindop

Cecil B de Mille
Loved to give people a thrill,
But one supposes
He had a hell of a job picking Moses.

Rosemarie Rowley

François Truffaut,
Whilst reading a script for a film about a UFO,
On a creative whim
Directed 'Jules et Jim.'

Jim Lindop

Busby Berkeley
Did nothing starkly.
His choreography's lavish
And can still astonish and ravish.

Adam Horovitz

Nicolas Winding Refn
Made the film I just watched, which was effin'
Marvellous: called 'Pusher II'.
I recommend it to you.

Ian Duhig

Jacques Tati
Gets rather ratty
When people say
He's a French Will Hay.

Adam Horovitz

Stanley
Was manly:
As sensitive as a new brick,
As present as the future. That's Kubrick.

Katy Evans-Bush

King Vidor,
Deemed a field leader,
I thought was just grand
Till I saw his crap film from a book by Ayn Rand.

Ian Duhig

Martin Scorsese
Got very lazy;
In 'The Gangs of New York', he's
Told shedloads of porkies.

Ian Duhig

M Night Shyamalan?
I think it's by karma, man,
That his reputation declines.
We ought to have seen the Signs.

Andy Jackson

Peter Jackson
Got all Anglo Saxon
Directing Tolkien. Did he stop it?
Did he fuck! He's back with The Hobbit.

Adam Horovitz

John Sturges'
Career verges
On perfection. I'm agape
At his Great Escape.

Andy Jackson

Francis Ford Coppola
Made himself unpopular
When he rescripted Apocalypse Now. It left John Milius
Bilious.

Andy Jackson

Luchino Visconti
Saw 'The Full Monty',
Which he thought was vile,
Bar Robert Carlyle.

Ian Duhig

DW Griffith
Said 'It's no myth. If
You want to be the best patriot you can,
Join The Klan.'

Andy Jackson

Mack Sennet
As scripted by Alan Bennett:
All wistful charm and poise
With The Keystone Cops as The History Boys.

George Szirtes

Preston Sturges
Suffered from the most terrible urges.
In fact his whole life unravels
After Sullivan's Travels.

George Szirtes

Dario Argento
Never went lento;
Though he made Giallo,
His films weren't shallow.

Ian Duhig

Karel Reisz
Was not always nice:
His Saturday Night was followed by Sunday Morning.
Let this be a warning.

George Szirtes

Roman Polanski
Got really fancy
With his famous tracking shot over the Dakota.
But nicer? Not one iota.

Katy Evans-Bush

Darren Aronofsky
Is no Tarkovsky.
He made molehill from mountain
When he filmed The Fountain.

Adam Horovitz

Lee Chang-dong
Did no wrong
Filming 'Poetry'
(Though he'd know it 'Shi').

Ian Duhig

Sergey Dvortsevoy
Brought me lots of joy:
Funny and tragic,
'Tulpan' is magic!

Ian Duhig

Edward Dmytryk
Never worked with Dietrich,
Though in a remake he did manage to mangle
Der Blaue Engel.

George Szirtes

Miike
Is friike;
'Gozu'
Is a very far cry from Ozu.

Ian Duhig

Wes Craven
Did not film The Raven,
And with his very last breath
Refused to direct The Masque of the Red Death.

George Szirtes

Mike Leigh
Is likely
To do better than 'Happy-Go-Lucky'
Which was yucky.

Ian Duhig

Clint Eastwood
Even when deceased would
Insist he
Be allowed to Play Misty.

George Szirtes

Quentin Tarantino
Spent far too long in the Kino.
Although the critics think he's groovy
All his ideas are stolen from other movies.

Andy Jackson

Satyajit Ray
I think rhymes with 'sky'
Though I'm fearful to say
It might just be 'ray'.

Ian Duhig

Murderers

John Reginald Halliday Christie
Was not a man to go out and get pissed. He
Immured his victims at 10 Rillington Place
And was a thorough disgrace.

Jim Lindop

Ruth Ellis
Asked, 'What the hell is
Going on? You can't hang a bird!'
But nobody heard.

Jim Lindop

Dennis Nilsen
Was addicted to Pilsen
And was often to be found
Buying the very last round.

George Szirtes

Phil Spector:
He wrecked a
Few lives. Sure left 'em reelin'
When he lost that lovin' feelin'.

Robert Fitzmaurice

Ronnie Kray
Liked to say
He only killed his own sort and no other
And insisted that he was kind to his mother.

Graham Mummery

Cain,
After his brother was slain,
Tried to shake off the 'world's first murderer' label,
But he just wasn't Abel.

Mark Totterdell

Nick Cotton
Was thoroughly rotten
To the whole lot
Of EastEnders, even his dear old mum Dot.

Mark Totterdell

Doctor Crippen
Was on a ship in
Mid-Atlantic before
Being nabbed by the very long arm of the law.

Mark Totterdell

Bluebeard's
True beard's
Not blue, that's why
Those wives had to dye.

Mark Totterdell

Burke and Hare
Said 'It's so unfair!
Our arms and legs are aching!
This is a grave undertaking.'

Tom Deveson

Thomas Neill Cream
Devised a novel scheme
For sexual and moral reform –
Strychnine and chloroform.

Tom Deveson

Bonnie and Clyde
Leave me dry-eyed.
There's nothing glamorous
In being murderous and amorous.

Tom Deveson

Pretty Boy Floyd
Would be rather annoyed
To have dwindled to three words
In a song by The Byrds.

Tom Deveson

Ivan the Terrible
Said 'I find being terrible quite unbearable.
I resolve to follow the teachings of Buddha
And strive to be Ivan the Gooder.'

Jim Lindop

Macbeth
Of death
Would not talk:
'Hah! As if woods could walk!'

Robert Fitzmaurice

Jeffrey Dahmer
Considered it karma
Saying 'If you can't beat them,
Eat them.'

Andy Jackson

Ed Gein:
If you've ever seen
The Texas Chainsaw
Massacre, you'll know the score.

Andy Jackson

Mark Chapman
Got a bad rap, man.
He's more notorious than Gary Gilmore
Who killed more.

Andy Jackson

Mr Ted Bundy
Killed Monday to Sunday;
Even two in one day
If the ladies passed his way.

Tracey Herd

Nursery Rhymes & Fairy Tales

Goldilocks
Rarely thought outside the box
And, consequently, only ate
What was on the plate.

Andy Jackson

Rapunzel
Shuns all
Phone calls from Princes, and will always declare
'Sorry, I'm washing my hair.'

Andy Jackson

Little Jack Horner
Leafed through some porn, a
Gleam in his eye, and said 'My,
What a bad boy am I!'

Mark Totterdell

Little Bo-Peep
Wouldn't sleep
With Georgie Porgie,
But was fairly partial to the occasional orgy.

Jim Lindop

Humpty Dumpty,
What a numpty!
Getting so smashed is eggstremely
Unseemly.

Mark Totterdell

Old King Cole
Was a merry old soul;
Young King Cole
Was an utter arsehole.

Paul McGrane

Jack the Giant Killer
Starred in an X-rated thriller
Doing something improper
With his little chopper.

Tom Deveson

Doctor Foster
Went to Gloucester
One wet morning,
Ignoring the Environment Agency's severe puddle warning.

Mark Totterdell

Rumpelstiltskin
Was wracked with guilt. 'Spin
Straw into gold? Pshaw,
I thought you said spin gold into straw.'

Andy Jackson

Cinderella
Couldn't attract a fella.
Always putting out, she never got a thing back
Until she discovered the Perspex slingback.

Andy Jackson

Wee Willie Winkie
Poured another drinkie.
He wasn't well hung
But the night was still young.

Robert Fitzmaurice

The Handsome Prince
Didn't so much strut as mince.
Said Snow White:
'Where can I get a REAL man this time of night?'

Andy Jackson

'Sleeping Beauty,
You're such a cutie!'
Thought the prince as he kissed her. I'm sure he meant
To get her consent.

Mark Totterdell

The Ugly Duckling
Said 'My resolve is buckling.
It's spring, but I can't figure
Why I'm still ugly, only bigger.'

Andy Jackson

Jack
Is Back
In Giant Killer 2! Book now!
More beans! More gold! More cow!

George Szirtes

Solomon Grundy,
Born on Sunday.
The midwife said 'You're
A tad premature.'

Andy Jackson

Jack Sprat
Has run to fat.
Exercise? He will not try it.
I recommend a low-cholesterol diet.

Andy Jackson

Jack and Jill
Seem to have taken a spill
And upset a perfectly good pail.
Mark that a fail.

George Szirtes

Baby Bunting
Was overheard grunting
'Tell my next of kin
I don't want no stinking rabbit skin.'

Tom Deveson

The Queen of Hearts
Said 'Where are my tarts?'
The Knave said 'Don't be silly,
They've gorn up the 'Dilly.'

Tom Deveson

The Snow Queen
Has often been
Depicted as malicious.
But why? Her ice cream is delicious.

George Szirtes

Little Boy Blue
Considered his hue
As he lay on the turf;
'Am I a Na'vi or am I a Smurf?'

Mark Totterdell

Tweedledum
Said 'What's to become
Of Tweedledee?
He's deutero-me.'

Tom Deveson

The Troll
Has no soul
But dotes
On goats.

George Szirtes

The Three Blind Mice
By an unprecedented rhetorical device
Persuaded the farmer's wife
To put down her knife.

Tom Deveson

Noddy
Hid the body,
But here comes PC Plod
And the Flying Squad.

Robert Fitzmaurice

Big Ears
Thought of himself as akin to the 'One and Only Billy Shears.'
But his version of 'Drive My Car, Noddy'
Was shoddy.

Jim Lindop

Tom Thumb
Said 'I'm not dumb,
I won't linger
Anywhere near Fred Finger.'

Tom Deveson

Mary Mary,
Far from being contrary,
Was actually so nice
They named her twice.

Mark Totterdell

The Giant
Was not compliant
With any food regulations I've ever read.
Ground bones aren't a permitted ingredient in bread.

Mark Totterdell

Jack's mother
Looked in the sky and said 'Another
Disaster! This means
You and I are has-beans.'

Tom Deveson

Little Miss Muffet
Decided to rough it,
Shunning all gluten and whey.
She lasted a day.

Alvin Pang

The third Brother Grimm –
Why haven't we heard of him?
His 'Once upon a time'
Was done in mime.

Tom Deveson

The Mouse
Lived in a confused house,
With a malfunctioning clock
That went Hockory-Chicory-Cock.

Andy Jackson

Old Mother Hubbard
Found sod-all in the cupboard.
These benefit cuts
Are harsh on poor mutts.

Mark Totterdell

Little Red Riding Hood
Reasoned her way out of the wood
Demonstrating the evolutionary gulf
Between human and wolf.

Andy Jackson

Little Tommy Tucker
Is a horrid little fucker.
He's terrible at singing
And his little neck needs wringing.

Mark Totterdell

Little Tommy Tucker
Cried out for succour
After such libellous remarks
In that clerihew of Mark's.

Tom Deveson

Goosey Goosey Gander
Admitted with candour
'I really have no excuse
For my gratuitous elderly abuse.'

Tom Deveson

The Old Woman Who Lived In A Shoe
Sought a judicial review
When nothing came
Of her child benefit claim.

Tom Deveson

Hansel and Gretel
Ate all
Of the witch's cottage, brick by candy brick,
And were spectacularly, extravagantly sick.

Mark Totterdell

Rock-a-bye Baby
Said 'Maybe
I'll get compensation
For my mother's lax attitude to a Health and Safety regulation.'

Tom Deveson

Robin Hood
Never understood
Why people laughed at the spoonerism of Friar Tuck.
But that was his bad luck.

Jim Lindop

An Ugly Sister,
Once you've kissed her,
Will probably reveal the splendour
Of his/her gender.

Andy Jackson

Johnny Appleseed
Noticed that America was untreed.
So he sowed
And they growed.

Jim Lindop

Tristan
Wouldn't listen
When Isolde
Complained about her chilblains now that the weather was
getting so much colder.

Jim Lindop

Mary
Was slightly wary
When the dinner lady said 'Your lamb's welcome of course!
Now, where did I put the mint sauce...?'

Robert Lindsay Marcus

The Little Mermaid,
If only she were made
With human legs and a fish's head;
That's a tale I'd love to have read.

Mark Totterdell

Bambi
May have been nambypamby,
But I bet you had something in your eye
When you saw his mother die.

Harry Gallagher

The Three Billy Goats Gruff,
Having had enough
Of trolls, and feeling bitter,
Deleted their accounts on Twitter.

Mark Totterdell

Puss in Boots?
The sane world disputes
Any tale that is premised
On a cat at the chemist.

Mark Totterdell

The Cow
Didn't get to explain how
She'd achieved the bovine moon-shot of the century
Before sizzling up on re-entry.

Mark Totterdell

Playwrights

John Osborne
Was born
In a kitchen sink,
Which was significant, I think.

Andy Jackson

Christopher Marlowe
Didn't write about Clarissa Harlowe.
If he had done,
She'd have been stabbed before the end of Act One.

Tom Deveson

Arnold Wesker
Said 'Est-ce que
Je puis manger avec vous
Des frites avec tous?'

Tom Deveson

David Hare
Said 'I don't care
That my plays come more than close
To being predictable, self-righteous and verbose.'

Tom Deveson

Steven Poliakoff
I wish he would jolly fuck off,
With his portentous balls.
Just words. That's all.

Andy Jackson

Oscar Wilde
Had a wife, a child, and another child:
But sodomy, which the fuzz banned,
Made him not An Ideal Husband.

Bill Greenwell

Jean Racine
Developed a dance routine;
He would sashay
To 'Vénus tout entière à sa proie attachée.'

Tom Deveson

Georges Féydeau
Said 'Je will model ze Tour d'Eiffel wiz ze Play-doh
While rahding mah bahcycle.
Zat will be farcical.'

Tom Deveson

Noel Coward
Felt empowered
When his morning work was done
To go out in the midday sun.

Tom Deveson

Alan Bennett
Addressed the US Senate.
He said 'Ee,
I'd love some Tetley's tea.'

Tom Deveson

Alan Ayckbourn
Didn't like to make porn,
Preferring farce
To tits and arse.

Andy Jackson

Molière
Wrote 'Le Malade Imaginaire',
Which you might wrongly feel
Is about a duck that isn't real.

Mark Totterdell

Samuel Beckett
Said 'Oh feck it!
It's hard to be happy
When life's so Krappy!'

Mark Totterdell

If Harold Pinter
Went on the inter-
Net, he'd have found Pinterest
Of great interest.

Mark Totterdell

Bertolt Brecht
Is the echt
Thing. Few works are properer
Than 'The Threepenny Opera'.

Mark Totterdell

Ernie Wise,
In his considerable dramatic oeuvre, defies
Every theatrical convention. As Tynan observed, and I quote,
'Wise has studiously ignored every criticism what I wrote.'

Jim Lindop

Anton Chekhov
Was a heck of
A writer,
Though his plays could have been lighter.

Mark Totterdell

Francis Bacon
Has been taken
By otherwise intelligent people to have written Shakespeare's plays
Which never ceases to amaze.

Mark Totterdell

Eugene O'Neill
Sat, drunk, behind the wheel,
Embarking, to his passengers' dismay,
On a long night's journey into day.

Tom Deveson

Ray Cooney
Should give up soon. He
Surely senses
There can only be so many 'hilarious consequences'.

Andy Jackson

David Mamet
Cursed 'Oh, damn it!
I left the Stations of the Cross
Out of Glengarry Glen Ross.'

Tom Deveson

Eugene Ionesco
Wrote scathingly after visiting a branch of Tesco,
'The whole thing is but a massive folly,
And all who go there off their collective trolley!'

Jim Lindop

Euripides
Didn't put zip-a-dees
Or doo-dahs in his plays.
It simply wasn't done in those days.

Mark Totterdell

Peter Nichols
Said 'Oooh! That tickles!'
During – I'm afraid –
Privates on Parade.

Tom Deveson

Peter Shaffer –
He's the gaffer.
Anthony Shaffer
Is somewhat naffer.

Tom Deveson

Michael Frayn
Started a whispering campaign
Against someone who tried to cough
During Noises Off.

Tom Deveson

Dario Fo
Said 'No! No! No!
The Conservative Party
Is an offshoot of commedia dell'arte.'

Tom Deveson

Luigi Pirandello
Was the fellow
Responsible for the
Snappily-titled 'Six Characters in Search of an Author'.

Mark Totterdell

Edward Albee
Shall be
Forever known for the gulf
Between everything else he wrote and 'Who's Afraid of Virginia Woolf?'.

Andy Jackson

Harold Brighouse
Bought a big house
And a Rolls Royce
With the proceeds of 'Hobson's Choice'.

Mark Totterdell

Plautus
Is about as
Old as Roman comic dramatists get.
I haven't googled him yet.

Mark Totterdell

Plautus –
According to the Latin teacher who taught us –
Is pronounced thus,
But I'm not making a fuss.

Tom Deveson

Steven Berkoff
Is a jerk of
The highest order, a complete waste of space,
Though I wouldn't say that to his face.

Mark Totterdell

George Bernard Shaw
Forbore,
After much persuasion from his editor,
From writing 'Pygmalion versus Predator'.

Mark Totterdell

Henrik Ibsen
Didn't exactly tell fibs'n
Lies,
But he did tend to dramatise.

Mark Totterdell

Poets

Philip Larkin
Insisted on seeing the dark in
Everything, the miserably contrarian
Librarian.

Mark Totterdell

Pablo Neruda's
Twenty poems were a little lewder
Than anything long
Written by Patience Strong.

James Sutherland Smith

Seamus Heaney
Rose so peerless and clean, he
Defied belief: no brown-nosing, no bitterness, no rage...
Not even a Facebook page.

Mark Granier

Alfred Lord Tennyson
Ate strong meat, including venison,
Of which, in season, he used to eat a lot
With roast potatoes and the Gravy of Shallot.

Simon Williams

Stevie Smith
Encouraged the myth
That she wasn't waving.
She's raving.

Andy Jackson

Wendy Cope
Loves sex, and a good soap.
Her foreplay involves watching Eastenders
In her suspenders.

Andy Jackson

John Greenleaf Whittier
Was as talented as JR Lowell. And prettier,
But one should not be too hard,
On a less than pretty bard.

George Szirtes

John Keats
Never washes his sheets,
And the clothes of Lord Byron
Never see an iron.

Andy Jackson

WB Yeats
Kept asking Maud Gonne for dates.
He said 'Aw, c'mon, let's get laid
In a bee-loud glade.'

Tom Deveson

Federico García Lorca
Wasn't much of a talker,
But what verse grew roots
Beneath the jackboots.

Robert Fitzmaurice

Sylvia Plath
Demanded 'Hath
Anyone seen my Muse,
Or hath she run off with Ted Hughes?'

George Szirtes

Gary Snyder
That great Beat outsider
Reoriented his pen
When he got into Zen.

Adam Horovitz

Anon
What are you on?
Your output sure puts mine to shame
I'm thinking I should change my name.

Joan Lennon

Ezra Pound
Was distressed when he found
His Pisan Cantos
Had been turned into pantos.

Colin Will

John Betjeman,
I wish I'd met ya, man:
I've not been so sorry yet
About not meeting any other Laureate.

Robert Lindsay Marcus

Andrew Motion
As Laureate made quite a commotion,
Which is why he is famous
But not as Nobel as Seamus.

Meg Cox

Geoffrey Hill
Had a surprise in Brazil.
After eight caipirinhas and seven glasses of Pimm's
He preferred the Portuguese translation of Mercian Hymns.

Tom Deveson

Gillian Clarke
Said 'Are the Arts Council having a lark?
For their next reading all the National Poets have to go
To Llanfairpwllgwyngyllgogerychwyrndrobwllllantysiliogogogoch?'

Tom Deveson

Geoffrey Chaucer
Found his language became coarser –
Right off the Whitehouse Scale –
When the Miller told his Tale.

Tom Deveson

Sir Thomas Wyatt
Led a life of disquiet –
It's not clever, if you value your skin,
To have it off with Anne Boleyn.

Tom Deveson

Edmund Spenser
Annoyed the censor
By adding an obscene
Addendum to The Faerie Queene.

Tom Deveson

Percy Bysshe Shelley
Had a hole in his right wellie.
To dry his soaking sock, he asked his buddy Byron
If he'd turn the bloody gas fire on.

Jim Lindop

Ted Hughes
Had some dodgy views
That he would sermonize and spout –
Nothing to Crow about.

Tom Deveson

Thom Gunn
Had a bit of fun
Asking Philip Larkin whether
He liked leather.

Tom Deveson

Christina Rossetti
Said 'Please, no confetti.
There's nothing odd
About only marrying God.'

Tom Deveson

John Milton
Bought some expensive Stilton,
With cheese-mites omitted from the cost –
Parasites Lost.

Tom Deveson

Bob Dylan?
Poet? Folk singer? Rock Villain?
You choose.
I'm too tangled up in The Blues.

Jim Lindop

Walt Whitman
Wrote some cool shit, man!
He had such class,
I want to smoke his Leaves of Grass!

Mark Totterdell

Edward, RS, Dylan;
I could fill an
Entire anthology with poets named Thomas,
But I won't, I promise.

Mark Totterdell

RS Thomas
Hated commas.
He claimed it was the English nation
To blame for evil punctuation.

George Szirtes

Alexander Pope
Had given up all hope.
He said 'I'm not going to queue
To see that harridan, Montagu.'

George Szirtes

Wystan Hugh Auden
Became a traffic warden
Who worked in Gloucester, Worcester and Leicester
But never in Chester.

Tom Deveson

Georg Trakl
Would often cackle
At the finer
Points of Heine.

George Szirtes

William Wordsworth
Said 'Even a turd's worth
Writing about, you see,
As long as it's written about by me!'

Mark Totterdell

Carol Ann Duffy?
I've had enough. We
All need a bit of poetry in our life,
But not the world and his wife.

Andy Jackson

Robert Browning
Was always clowning.
He even tried to get a camel in
The Pied Piper of Hamelin.

George Szirtes

John Donne;
Bet he's been done,
But only in the metaphysical sense.
Each sonnet costs six hundred pence.

Robert Fitzmaurice

Louis MacNeice
Longed for some peace.
He looked at the snow.
Did that bring peace? No.

George Szirtes

Dante Alighieri
Was regarded as a bit of a fairy
In Italy,
Which he regretted bitterly.

Jim Lindop

Erich Fried
Was very cross indeed
And vehemently denied
He was Erich Fried.

Imogen Forster

Charles Baudelaire,
Malgré son esprit de 'laisser-faire'
Se trouvait toujours pris de vertige
Quand il voyait chaque fleur vibrant sur sa tige.

Jim Lindop

Paul Verlaine
Stood in the rain.
It rained in his heart.
He did it for art.

Imogen Forster

William McGonagall
Was derided by one and all.
But here's the news:
Because they scan badly and have forced rhymes he would
have been a natural when it came to clerihews.

Andy Jackson

William McGonagall
Should not be thought canonical.
His verse reads like the epitome
Of everything that's shit to me.

Mark Totterdell

William McGonagall
Despite Mark Totterdell
Wrote the best poem about a bridge disaster on the River Tay
I have seen to this day.

Simon Williams

William Langland
Felt the pang and
Wrote Piers Plowman,
But he's long dead now, man.

Andy Jackson

Arthur Hugh Clough
Said 'Enough's enough.
It's quite unfair
To say I despair.'

Imogen Forster

ee cummings
unpublished hummings
will shortly be published in a book
just l(oo)k

George Szirtes

Pam Ayres'
Poetry wares
Are quite sorry, yet
She's better known than the Poet Laureate.

Andy Jackson

TE Hulme
We must assume
Breathed his last
In BLAST.

George Szirtes

Rosemary Tonks.
It's been yonks!
Last seen writing in a shed.
Possibly dead.

Rachel Rooney

Thomas Hood
Was always doing good
And was ever alert
To the song of a shirt.

George Szirtes

EJ Thribb
Would rarely ad-lib,
Starting each poem with 'So, farewell then...',
All other openings being beyond his ken.

Andy Jackson

Anon
Kept going on and on
Until everyone was shattered.
Who was he? It hardly mattered.

George Szirtes

Edith Sitwell
Would fit well
Into her own book of English Nutters.
Part screams, part mutters.

George Szirtes

Rumi
Was seldom gloomy.
Just because he was a Sufi
Didn't mean he couldn't be goofy.

George Szirtes

Arthur Rimbaud,
Said 'I am who I am, bro.
You think I'm your brother,
But je est another.'

George Szirtes

Catullus
Shouldn't lull us
Into thinking of the purity of heaven –
See: Poem XCVII.

Tom Deveson

Zbigniew Herbert,
Who loved lemon sherbet,
Found the only bar to his fame
Was nobody knew how to pronounce his forename.

Graham Mummery

John Burnside
Has his stern side,
But with every prize he wins,
He grins and grins and grins.

Mark Totterdell

Wallace Stevens
Said 'The odds are evens
When I rise from my writing bench
Whether the poem's English or French.'

Tom Deveson

Robert Herrick
Was a mite too randy for a cleric.
Even Julia
Thought it peculiar.

George Szirtes

Thomas Nashe
Said 'Sorry, luvvies, must dash.
Due for drinks in Eaton Square
And brightness falls from the air.'

Tom Deveson

Abelard
Tried hard
To win Heloise's heart, though
He found it harder as a castrato.

Rachel Rooney

Henry Reed
Said 'One thing I don't need –
When the rumpy-pumpy starts
I can do without Naming of Parts.'

Tom Deveson

Anne Sexton
Was supposed to have written a text on
A Sexton called Blake,
But it's a fake.

George Szirtes

Rainer Maria Rilke
Always wanted to milk a
Prizewinning dairy cow
But didn't know how.

Graham Mummery

Dorothy Parker
Wrote with a felt marker
Of the big fat sort.
That's why her poems are short.

George Szirtes

Nahum Tate
Wasn't great
And is hardly worth defending –
But he did give Lear a happy ending.

George Szirtes

Alfred Noyes
Employs
Nominative indecisiveness;
'I'm Alfred No...yes'.

Mark Totterdell

Martial
Was partial
To spring lambs
And epigrams.

Karen Margolis

Robert Frost
Once got lost.
He was mistaken
About the road not taken.

Michael Rosen

William Blake
Could give and take.
If his poems didn't sell
He could draw as well.

Karen Margolis

Emily Dickinson.
With her it's slim pickin's on
Ways to punctuate –
She was always dashing – and wouldn't wait.

Joan Lennon

Henry Wadsworth Longfellow
Was probably the wrong fellow
To have tried to be the author
Of Hiawatha.

Michael Rosen

Proverbials

Jean-Paul Sartre
Sat at his usual table in the Café des Sports in Montmartre.
He took a sip of his drink, smiled the smile of a sated anaconda,
And pronounced that absinthe made the Sartre grow fonder.

Jim Lindop

Stéphane Mallarmé
Liked to dress in second-hand foil and lamé,
But he should have been told
That all that's Gary Glitter's is not gold.

Andy Jackson

Neville Chamberlain
Never saw the danger in
Appeasement. Maybe he had to go,
But sometimes it's better the Neville you know.

Andy Jackson

Fred Astaire
Was just half of a pair.
True, Ginger and Cyd were less well-known,
But man does not live by Fred alone.

Andy Jackson

Michael Palin
Said 'My satnav is failin'.
I'm supposed to be going to Macedonia
But I can't get out of bloody Estonia.'

Andy Jackson

Edouard Manet
Sat on his favourite bench in the Jardins des Tuileries, reading
The Adventures of Richard Hannay.
He dozed off and walkers began to peep
At the famous painter, murmuring 'There's Manet asleep....'

Jim Lindop

Giorgio Locatelli
Grew a sizeable belly
After several overeating disasters,
Proving no man can serve two pastas.

Andy Jackson

André Gide
Laid down plenty of feed,
But his cook was well goosed:
All his chickens came home to Proust.

Robert Fitzmaurice

Gustave Flaubert
Sprang from his satin to go bare,
But despite a well-placed waffle
Too many cocks spoil the brothel.

Robert Fitzmaurice

Thomas Edison
Yawned and went to bed. His son
And German friends would then smirk,
As many Hans make light work.

Robert Fitzmaurice

Tutankhamun
Died far too soon.
He may have grown up to be proud and haughty
But nobody loves a pharaoh when he's forty.

Andy Jackson

Jay-Z
Came round for tea
But only stayed a minute, though.
Jay-Z come, Jay-Z go.

Andy Jackson

Tom Baker
Is a bit of a troublemaker,
But is allergic to fruit, so hey!
An apple a day keeps The Doctor away.

Andy Jackson

Aneurin Bevan
Went to the dentists at eleven.
The dentist, who was a joker in his youth,
Said 'Ah! Nye for a Nye, and a tooth for a tooth.'

Andy Jackson

Brian Cox
(Astrophysicist not actor) turned up with a box
Which turned out to be empty. I was a little miffed,
So I say 'Beware geeks bearing gifts'.

Andy Jackson

George Osborne
Was drawn
In such a style that it revealed his inner glory,
For every picture sells a Tory.

Andy Jackson

David Lloyd George,
Apart from knowing my father, was known to have stayed at
an Inn near The Cheddar Gorge.
The innkeeper recognised him and asked a passer-by
How to address the great man. He replied 'Never say Dai!'

Jim Lindop

Russian Leaders

Joseph Stalin
Was nobody's darlin'
When he felt the urge
For a purge.

Andy Jackson

Yuri Andropov
Would often take his top off
In a Politburo meeting
On account of the heating.

Andy Jackson

Vyacheslav Molotov
Threw a cocktail party but had to call it off.
When Zinoviev set fire to Stalin's hair,
It proved to be an incendiary affair.

Andy Jackson

Nikita Khruschev
Said 'I'm rushed off
My feet. All those state marches!'
He being a martyr to his fallen arches.

Andy Jackson

Leonid Brezhnev
Appeared on Master Chef.
'What ingredients will I use?
Kasha, intellectuals, borscht and Jews.'

Tom Deveson

Lavrentiy Beria
Was like an ogre, but scarier.
His NKVD
Was no NYPD.

Colin Will

Iosif Dzhugashvili
Knew it would be silly
To keep his Georgian name.
Stalin, man of steel, was assured of fame.

Susan Jordan

Vladimir Putin
Likes to put the boot in
And is being terribly insular
Over the Crimean peninsula.

Brian Joyce

Scientists & Inventors

John Logie Baird
Never cared
Much for Alexander Graham Bell. He
Preferred watching his telly.

Andy Jackson

Alexander Graham Bell
Said 'Well,
If Baird prefers to be left alone
I won't bother to phone.'

Andy Jackson

Richard G Drew
May mean nothing to you;
A man so horribly out of shape
He had to invent masking tape.

George Szirtes

James Prescott Joule
Fiddled with heat and fuel.
He worked so hard to fine-tune it,
He became an energy unit.

David Hill

Thomas Crapper
Over there, looking dapper.
You'd hardly know he's a broken man
Since his life went down the pan.

Andy Jackson

Gregor Mendel
Said 'This hybridization trend'll
Let you tell the sex of beans –
Take down their genes.'

Tom Deveson

Louis Braille
Despite the veil
Of blindness, freed
The blind to read.

Shauna Robertson

Ray Dolby
Is someone we should all be
Grateful to.Though one of the boys,
He was never a big noise.

Andy Jackson

Karl Friedrich Benz
Didn't have many friends.
He invented Mercedes
To get in with the ladies.

Paul McGrane

Louis Pasteur
Was known to err
About germs and other things of that ilk,
Checking for them in his glass of milk.

Graham Mummery

Stephen Hawking
Was uncommonly fond of stalking
God; his eventual goal
To bury Him in the original black hole.

Mark Granier

Sir Clive Sinclair
Calculates in his chair
That it moves and is alive.
Oh no! It's a C5.

Graham Mummery

Hermann Rorschach
Took some flak,
Not only blotting his copybook,
But shouting hysterically 'Look!'

Mark Granier

Hedy Lamarr
The golden age star
Was startlingly pioneering
In communications engineering.

Helen Ivory

Linus Pauling
Had a triple calling –
DNA; CND;
And – alas – Vitamin C.

Tom Deveson

Whitcomb Judson
Came up with the goods one
Day, inventing the zip on a whim.
There were no flies on him.

Andy Jackson

Christopher Cockerell
Went off his rocker. Well
Almost, when he got the note:
'Is this a plane... or a boat?'

Robert Fitzmaurice

The Lord
Said 'Oh My Gawd
Would Dawkins be missed
If he didn't exist?'

Paul McGrane

Georg Ohm
Said 'I have to go home,
But I'll need some assistance –
There's too much resistance.'

Tom Deveson

Niels Bohr
Was smuggled to Scotland during the war.
His ideas met with unfamiliarity:
'We dinnae ken yon Complementarity.'

Tom Deveson

Paul Dirac
Went to pubs for the craic.
He loved a boozy natter
About antimatter.

Tom Deveson

Heinrich Hertz
Has got his deserts.
Posterity raves –
The applause comes in waves.

Tom Deveson

Caractacus Potts
Invented lots,
But dang!
He'll only ever be known for Chitty Chitty Bang Bang.

Paul McGrane

Max Planck
Looked completely blank.
'What's a photon?
Er...I'll put me coat on.'

Tom Deveson

Alan Turing
Was reassuring.
He claimed 'I'm no code crusader,
For the love of Ada.'

Simon Williams

Wilf Lunn
Had tons of fun
Making surreal cycles
With outrageous titles.

Kevin Reid

Robert Van DeGraaff
Is not to be found in any photograph.
There he stands by his generator
But is gone a moment later.

George Szirtes

Konrad Lorenz
Made numerous friends
Amongst nidifugous geese. Later,
They called him Mater.

Rachel Rooney

Professor Yaffle
Invented naff all.
But don't make a fuss;
Neither did Bagpuss.

Paul McGrane

Tim Berners-Lee
Means nothing to me.
Of what he invented I'm unaware.
Google him if you want. I don't care.

Andy Jackson

Boulton and Watt?
They weren't so hot,
But Richard Trevithick,
Now, he was terrific.

Andy Jackson

The fourth Earl of Sandwich
Always had one hand which
Was holding meat, the other bread.
'There's got to be an integrated solution that would release
synergies,' he said.

David Hill

Albert Einstein
When umpiring always used the same line
When the bowling side appealed:
'Ah! A unified field.'

James Sutherland Smith

Erwin Schrödinger
Was observed herding a
Load of cats into a box.
Why? It's a paradox.

Mark Totterdell

Archimedes,
It's agreed, he's
The one who yelled 'Eureka!'
And became the world's first streaker.

Mark Totterdell

Robert Oppenheimer
Couldn't stop in time, or
Halt his colleagues going all out,
Which led to fallout.

Andy Jackson

Peter Higgs
Endured many good-natured digs
From his children, asking 'Have you found the boson?'
He would answer 'No, son.'

Andy Jackson

Edward Teller
Was a decent feller,
Always kind to his mom,
He went down a bomb.

Andy Jackson

The Irish

Jonathan Swift
Possessed a rare gift.
But it all unravelled
After Gulliver travelled.

Andy Jackson

Joseph Locke
Liked a bit of heavy rock
And almost joined Led Zeppelin when a
Call went out for a ballsy tenor.

Andy Jackson

WB Yeats
Was adept at juggling plates,
His turn being the highlight
Of the Celtic Twilight.

George Szirtes

Bram Stoker
Was a bit of a joker.
The current mania for vampire novels rests on his shoulder.
Well, at least he is a stake-holder.

Andy Jackson

Sheridan Le Fanu
Never knew
How long his ghost stories would last on the shelf.
Now he's made a spectre of himself.

Andy Jackson

Seamus O'Toole
Was nobody's fool.
But the blighter
Wasn't a writer.

Jim Lindop

Bernard MacLaverty
Understood the gravity
Of the situation with the UDA, UVF, IRA et al,
So wrote 'Cal'.

Andy Jackson

Oscar Fingal O'Flahertie Wills Wilde
Was a gifted child
But his life was not rosy
After drinking cider with Bosie.

Bill Greenwell

Samuel Barclay Beckett
Thought of life that religion would wreck it;
He was in the drama biz, then,
But he's also in Wisden.

Bill Greenwell

If Frank Carson
Had been Stieg Larsson
We would have rejoiced in his
'The Girl With the Pint Of Guinness'.

Bill Greenwell

Shane MacGowan;
Are we allowin'
Him in here? It's a farce.
He's Irish? Kiss my arse.

Andy Jackson

Jedward
(John and Edward)
Are rawful
(Rubbish and awful).

Mark Totterdell

Feargal Sharkey
Sang loads of malarkey
About teenage kicks.
Now he's pushing 56.

Mark Totterdell

Fionn mac Cumhaill
Was no fumhaill.
Sharp as a pionn
Was Fionn.

Mark Totterdell

Bob Geldof
Never held off
From speaking his mind. I'm not knocking
His use of the word 'focking'.

Mark Totterdell

Did Father Jack
Enjoy the craic?
Did he heck!
'DRINK! GIRLS! FECK!'

Mark Totterdell

Michael O'Leary
Has a money-making theory
That involves, as far as I can ascertain,
Passengers providing their own plane.

Andy Jackson

Barack O'Bama
Could have been an Offaly farmer;
He'd have had great craic
Suppin' tay and ayting brack.

Peadar O'Donoghue

Bertie Ahern
Could do a good turn
For any old dope
With a brown envelope.

Peadar O'Donoghue

Éamon de Valera
Would often share a
Pot of Earl Grey with Joseph Locke,
Which was something of a Taoiseach.

Andy Jackson

Roddy Doyle
Was no son of the soil,
Reckoning towns to be nice.
Well, just Barrytown to be precise.

Andy Jackson

Grace O'Malley,
Should you meet her up a dark alley,
Would probably give you a duffin'
If you tried to touch her muffin.

Peadar O'Donoghue

Edna O'Brien
And her first novel got a bit of a fryin',
But now in times more enlightened than then
She's the lauded doyenne.

Peadar O'Donoghue

Molly Malone
Aims to make me her own.
My cockles are warmed by her hustles,
But I think she just wants a man with mussels.

Andy Jackson

Flann O'Brien
Was frequently found tryin'
To put his bicycle in the larder
While crying 'Here's mud in yer Garda!'

WN Herbert

Van Morrison
Was heard to say to his drummer 'Sorry son,
Yer timing's sadly lacking.
What a marvellous night for a sacking.'

Andy Jackson

Orla Guerin
Will, I swear in
A minute, and for the first time in a while,
Smile.

Andy Jackson

George Best,
Rest
His soul,
Was a divvil for the goal.

Jim Lindop

Bono,
(Oh, no!)
Designed a whole new clothing collection –
F-E-C-K – The Irish Connection.

Jim Lindop

Willie John McBride
Was extremely tall and very wide.
His very presence in a maul
Would terrify opponents, one and all.

Jim Lindop

St Patrick
Converted Ireland to Christianity, drove out all the snakes, and,
for a hat-trick,
Admitted on The Confessional's rock-hard pew
That he was really Welsh and so should not really be in this clerihew.

Jim Lindop

George Bernard Shaw
Was red in tooth and claw,
But it was worse than anyone feared,
He was also red in beard.

George Szirtes

George Berkeley
Put it rather starkly:
The thing at which you stare
Is neither here nor there.

George Szirtes

Laurence Sterne
Could hardly wait his turn
With Tristram Shandy.
He was that randy.

George Szirtes

Cusacks;
One could fill quite a few sacks
With actors of that name
Who've achieved fame.

Mark Totterdell

St Colmcille
Said 'Saints alive, don't be silly –
I'm off to Iona.
And don't expect me to phone ya.'

WN Herbert

Charles Stewart Parnell
Said 'It's begun to swell.'
'Hip hip hooray!'
Said Kitty O'Shea.

Tom Deveson

John Millington Synge
Said 'Fey weeping girls are my thing.
What leaves me cold?
A Playboy of the Western World centrefold.'

Tom Deveson

Louis MacNeice
Wished for an increase –
However nefarious –
In the drunkenness of things being various.

Tom Deveson

St Brendan
Sailed to Hendon.
Silly chap
Had the wrong map.

Mark Totterdell

Nora Joyce
Was a woman of voice.
She talked round the town
While James wrote it all down.

Karen Margolis

Sean MacBride
Was his mother's pride.
She, praise the Lord,
Was the lovely Maud.

Karen Margolis

Christy Moore
Used to be poor
Till he sang Irish kitsch.
That soon made him rich.

Karen Margolis

Graham Norton
Is thought an
Acceptable chat show host
By some, not most.

Mark Totterdell

Frank McCourt
Thought
'Angela's Ashes?
That's where the cash is!'

Mark Totterdell

Chris O'Dowd
Starred in 'The IT Crowd'
Where he was only slightly less mardy
Than Richard Ayoade.

Mark Totterdell

Kenneth Branagh
Is handy with a spanagh.
He's starred in many tool-related films, old and new,
Like Shakespeare's Gimlet and The Aiming of the Screw.

Simon Williams

Television

Derek Trotter
Could often spot a
Business opportunity, genuine or hooky.
Be lucky, Del, be lucky!

Andy Jackson

Harold
Preferred to be nicely apparelled,
But Albert Steptoe
Was a scruffy klepto.

Bill Greenwell

Jerry
Would claim to be very
Happy with Margot, but he did harbour a
Bit of a thing for Barbara.

Mark Totterdell

Tom
Would never stray from
Barbara, but couldn't embargo
The occasional wild fantasy about Margot.

Mark Totterdell

Carrie
Wanted to marry
Mr Big. The plot
Dragged on till they tied the knot.

Karen Margolis

Mr Bean
Is always betwixt and between;
He's so gormless, he hasn't a clue,
Just like me. No, I mean you.

Tom Deveson

'Fletch
Makes me want to kvetch
And twine and greet and mither and cry,'
Said the idiomatically confused Mr Mackay.

Tom Deveson

Mr Barraclough
Said 'I've had enough.
Forgive my tirade
But I've had it up to here with Slade.'

Andy Jackson

Hyacinth Bouquet
Is always trying to convey
That her name isn't 'Bucket'.
Onslow just says 'Don't bother.'

Tom Deveson

Rigsby
Said 'Couldn't my digs be
Cleaner, less soggy,
Without this measly moggy?'

Robert Fitzmaurice

Father Dougal McGuire
Is someone I admire.
I hope
He's the next Pope.

Tom Deveson

Reginald Iolanthe Perrin
Hadn't a care in
The world until his midlife crisis.
He falls. He rises.

Andy Jackson

Albert Arkwright
Would stay open until dark night.
Should Granville fall into sloth
He would be instructed to fer-fer-fetch his cloth.

Andy Jackson

Sybil –
Let's not quibble –
Didn't dazzle
Basil.

Mark Totterdell

Frank Spencer
In his defence, a
Better man than many here
In that he acted without fear.

Andy Jackson

Hancock
Never dreamed of Bangkok:
You don't dream
In East Cheam.

Bill Greenwell

Harry Worth
Used to mirror his girth
In shop windows. Oh what a bitter pill
That now we only have Harry Hill.

Robert Fitzmaurice

Private Sponge
Made the occasional lunge
Towards Dad's Army glory,
But seldom figured in the story.

Mark Totterdell

Wolfie Smith
Was the truth behind the myth
Of Maoist recruiting
In 1970's Tooting.

Mark Totterdell

Muffin the Mule –
Remember him and you'll
Be as old as the hills,
Like his pal, Annette Mills.

Sharon Larkin

Malcolm Tucker
– Scary fucker –
Spun the lot
Then lost the plot.

Sarah Walker

Doctor Kildare
(I longed to be in his care) –
The sexiest of the docs
Ever seen on the box.

Sharon Larkin

Emma Peel
(Leather jumpsuit, knee-highs, heels).
John Steed (short and fat,
Rolled umbrella, bowler hat).

Sharon Larkin

Number Six,
Found himself in a fix,
Dodging opalescent spheres
In Portmeirion, for years.

Sharon Larkin

Inspector Morse
Of the Thames Valley Force
Drank beer and solved his crossword as
Sergeant Lewis solved the murders.

Judi Sutherland

US Politics

Dwight David Eisenhower
Has a lot to say about the rising power
Of the Communist Bloc. It's
Mostly about rockets.

Andy Jackson

Teddy Roosevelt
Often felt
A twinge in his chest
Where the bullet was lodged. Wear a vest.

Shauna Robertson

James K Polk
Was one of those down-home country folk
Who played a mean fiddle on call.
Yee-haw! Y'all!

Jim Lindop

Franklin Delano Roosevelt
Sometimes wore a looser belt,
And in tropical places
Just relied on his braces.

Andy Jackson

Sarah Palin;
If she has a failin',
It's probably this:
Everything she is.

Andy Jackson

Lyndon Baines Johnson
Was told 'Kennedy's gone, son,
And now we demand a
New Supreme Commander.'

Andy Jackson

William Howard Taft
Wrote 'Calling Occupants of Interplanetary Craft'
For The Carpenters. His song
Got them a Number One Hit...no, wait a minute...that's wrong!

Jim Lindop

Chester A Arthur
Had a secret and long-held desire to bath a
Young woman in asses milk,
Accompanied by Acker Bilk.

Jim Lindop

Ulysses S Grant
Would love to dance but he can't,
Whereas Herbert Hoover
Is quite a mover.

Andy Jackson

Bill Clinton
Tried the ozone at Frinton,
But to no avail –
He didn't inhale.

Tom Deveson

John Tyler
Became a crossword compiler.
His most successful clue? –
'President Who?'

Tom Deveson

Andrew Jackson
Was a bit lax on
The punishment of people who disrespected his name.
I would not have done the same.

Andy Jackson

Jimmy Carter
Was smarter
Than the average bear.
But a second term? He hadn't a prayer.

Grant Tarbard

Richard Nixon
Would often get his kicks on
Hearing recorded conversations,
Hence the word 'buggeration'.

Andy Jackson

Bobby Kennedy.
This is a poor threnody
For what might have been.
A meagre clerihew paean.

Adam Horovitz

Barack Obama
Is quite the charmer.
Next, Michelle?
Only time will tell.

Jacqueline Saphra

JFK
Wa-hey!
Some liked it hot;
Some others got shot.

Robert Fitzmaurice

Donald Trump
Took an almighty dump
Only to find
It came out his mind.

Tom Deveson

George W Bush
Had such a huge crush
On Tony Blair,
They had a foreign affair.

Harry Gallagher

Harry S Truman
In 1945 was the new man.
I'd like to read more about him but I fear
The book stops here.

Andy Jackson

The Editors

Andy Jackson
Lacks an
Artistic sensibility, and one or two social graces
But shouldn't be dismissed solely on that basis.

George Szirtes
Is not to be confused with either John or Robert Surtees.
One drove cars, the other rode to hounds.
The similarity is merely in the sounds.